psychodynamically designed II

E.L.

ISBN-13: 978-1-718-06102-6
ISBN-10: 1-718-06102-X

This book is dedicated to each and every one of my readers. I am grateful and will forever cherish your support. I hope the words on these pages inspire each of you, in the same ways you all inspire me.

I want to take the time to genuinely apologize
to those I've hurt while facing my own pain
I now realize that I've been in the wrong
by continuing such a vicious cycle

Pineapples are my favorite
although I'm slightly allergic..
and I know better not to eat them,
yet I continue to consume
sort of similar to my feelings for you
I know better not to love you,
but here I am - still blatantly consumed by you

Emptiness on a very different level
so empty that your stomach rumbles in pain
but no substance will provide a filling sensation
and so you allow each rumble to pass
as your skin sinks closer to your bones
in hopes the end result will merely consist of
a reflection you can love, or even just accept

In my opinion, I think the worst emotion a person can experience is numbness - when you completely stop feeling anything at all

They say I'm a charmer and a flirt - that I have a way with words that draw people in and cause them to fall. If they only knew how much pain my words have caused, how many souls I've damaged, and the amount of hearts I've broken by stringing together words that just sounded good at the time, yet lacked any meaning.. I've learned my lesson, but the guilt still haunts me with each passing day.

I cannot stand to witness people allowing compliments go to their heads so much that their egos grow like weeds leaving their souls and inner beauty neglected

Reaching out once every year
sometimes every two or three
is not how a parent shows love
sorry to disappoint you

Maybe make-up isn't really my thing because in the past
it never made me feel attractive or confident
I only ever used it to cover up bruises and pain

I never knew the fire inside of you burned so bright
until I watched your brown eyes turn to flames
we were so young bound to make mistakes
which resulted in your unique punishments
such as confinement to a chair using tape
I can still hear the shattering of glass
above our heads to this day
and all I have continued to wonder:
did we really drive you to rage...
or was it the demons in your head?

I aspire to be the type of person
that someone speaks passionately about to God

Most children growing up associate razors with shaving
my affiliation was always the color red
craving those sharp edges against my skin
because it was the only pain I could control

-the pain of the world no longer phased me

As children, we were constantly instructed
to drink plenty of milk to make our bones strong

Why did we never receive instruction
on how to strengthen our mentalities or souls?

Call me a fool or whatever you deem fit,
but even if I am never able to call her mine,
my love for her will carry on,
in my mind she will forever exist

I developed an infatuation early in life
with lending a helping hand,
exchanging inspirational words,
and twenty-four years later..
it has bloomed into a passionate devotion

To the next person that falls for me:

My hard ass exterior is just a defense mechanism truth be told, I'm
sensitive - very much so, in fact
My smile is just my way of hiding because I rarely admit when I am hurt
My laughs are not always sincere - they sometimes just bury my pain
My anger tends to get the best of me; unfortunately, I often take it out on
those who care and I tend to push everyone away

*Loving me will never be easy, **not by any means***

I am the first to admit that I am difficult to love,
but if you try your best to not give up on me,
you'll discover my true intentions - loving you wholeheartedly

I am not ashamed to admit that *I'm not okay*
& I haven't been for quite some time

Please remember: it is perfectly **okay** to *not be okay*.

So many people walk through life
sliding masks on and off,
as if each day is Halloween
when will we finally retire our disguises
and reveal our true faces to the world?

-Do not <u>ever</u> be scared to simply be YOU.

We face so many challenges and overcome numerous obstacles in attempts to hide our pain from anyone on the outside looking in. Yet, we fail to recognize and come to terms with the damage that lingers within us, the pain that no make-up can conceal. Truth is, when we face that very pain within ourselves, we open opportunities to truly free ourselves from the emotional chains that we never imagined we could break.

If you ever find yourself giving up and giving in, standing closer to the edge, please remember that I will put my problems and pain aside to ensure you keep pushing through life because **your life is important to me.**

Watching someone you love kill herself slowly with each swallow
and still loving her just the same, if not more.
Staying with someone who mentally abuses you
because you still believe deep down they're a good person.
Hiding your personal struggles and pain
in order to ensure those around you are taken care of.
Putting the razor or knife down
instead of allowing it to slide across your skin.
Not ending your own life because it would only pass along the pain
to those who care about you, those who deserve happiness.
Placing your feelings aside for someone you've fallen in love with
because you know it will be less complicated for them.

- *What is strength?*

I cannot emphasize enough that tomorrow is **NOT** guaranteed for **ANY** of us!! Whatever you've been wanting to do, do it **NOW**.

I believe in you.

We played questions like how we used to back in middle school:

"What do you notice about a person first?"

Smiles was her reply

I found her response so ironic, though, because while she is attracted to the ones around her, she seems to fail at noticing her own..

shed, but do not forget entirely - our pasts, like snake skin

Dear Future Child(ren),

Please don't ever hesitate to tell me anything - your feelings, your dreams, your fears, even your mistakes. No matter how ambitious, dark, or scary, I **will** support you regardless! I will **always** be your biggest fan in life, through the ups and the downs. I will **not** give up on you and more importantly, I will never let you give up on yourself! These are just some (with many more to come) of my promises to you.

I strive to discover the parts of a person the universe has yet to see

She may understand my level of desire
to spend the rest of my days discovering
all that life has to offer,
but I'm certain she does not know
my level of desire to spend the rest of my days
making those discoveries with *her*.

Far too often, closed doors conceal harsh realities

punches

yelling

rape

neglect

I pray this does not apply to the one reading these pages

On Sunday you won't see me at church
I can't remember the last time a hymn crossed my lips
I'm not proud of my lack of religious expression
I'm not the perfect Christian by any means
and it may be unnoticeable to those around me
but my faith is forever strong
because I know in my heart
He will always be the one I can turn to
when life knocks me to my knees
and I know he will be listening
when I bow my head and pray

The leaves are beginning to change
and will soon disappear
I, too, am changing
the person I've been
is following the leaves
but while there is confidence
that the leaves will return in Spring
I'm not so sure about me

<u>02 NOV - 1 AM</u>
The most honest she's ever been
even admitted to her own faults
which she rarely ever does
all while I caught myself
falling once again
this time harder than before
and in that same moment I was breaking
as I began to realize I'm too late

-I should have never taken you for granted

If my soul was dusted for fingerprints
a few different sets would likely be found
but I can guarantee hers appear the most
because no one has touched my soul
in the ways she has, time and time again

take my hand
walk through this life by my side
we've been given a second chance
and I want nothing more than to make it right..

At times, we only love a person out of habit, even if we are not truly *in* love. I will admit there was a point that I started to wonder if you were merely just a habit of mine and the actual love was gone. Well, it takes 21 days to break a habit they say and it's been several months.. So, I guess it is safe to say if you are in fact a habit, *you're the one I'll never break.*

They all crave who she is
when her clothes are on the floor
they only want her sexual side
believe me, I want that side of her too
but the side I crave the most
is the one she keeps hidden
the one the universe has yet to see

Although her physical body
is still standing on this earth
she is no longer alive
her heart may still be beating
and her lungs still pull in air
but her mind has committed suicide
her soul has turned dark and bare

Overlooking the valley as I attempt to focus
on self-reflection and peace of mind
both have always been difficult for me
because I never seem to stop and concern myself
about the most important person in my life:

ME

around you, my life's colors tend to shine a bit brighter
and my problems begin to fade away

they asked me to list my weaknesses
starting with my biggest
and with no hesitation
my list was introduced with *her*

I rarely have success in maintaining relationships
with those the same age as me
I often wonder if it's because they
have yet to reach a level of wisdom and maturity
a level I have already surpassed

Take me to the ocean under the stars
where I can lay in the cold sand,
feel the cool breeze, and close my eyes
as I absorb the rare aura of tranquility

Never have I been a lipstick and heels type of female. My outfits, more often than not, are compromised of black, but some days I do wear red. To remind myself and those surrounding me that I am a walking **red flag**.

proceed with caution

I hope you find someone who enraptures more than just your body
someone who also provides pleasure to your heart and soul

In my mind, sometimes writers
also have interest in photography
using pictures to replace the words
they fail to string together
in order to express their emotions

I am accustomed to the *never*-lasting
permanent aspects of my life ceased to exist
that was until you entered my journey
imprinting everlasting tracks on my heart

Dear you,

Please stop shutting situations out and avoiding reality! Open your eyes and face your fears. I know you don't understand why this is happening to you, but I know you can get through it! You are strong enough to do anything, but you have to believe in yourself as much as I believe in you. Most importantly, remember you are **not** alone.

We will get through this, **together.**

Elation brings a radiance to a person's face
that I strive to see on every face of the world

- Yes, you do deserve to be happy

With no explanation:

"I never want to lose you"

turned into

"Please leave me alone"

What did I do for you to hate me?

attempting to rid your demons will not prevail
while you carry on low-key enjoying the company they keep..

I keep finding random notes you wrote me
in almost every notebook and journal I come across
and with each one I read, a smile forms across my face
but I'd be lying if I said they didn't sting a bit, too

-I miss being loved by you

trying to hold up those around you
while hiding the madness of your own mind

-quickest way to destroy yourself

as we get older and time continues to pass,
change is constant; summer turns to winter,
friends walk away, babies are born,
and relationships either excel or end

yet, we constantly yearn change in our lives,
then turn around and fear it, but I think change
isn't even what we are so afraid of..

the true fear, I believe is settling down and life staying the same

There is no comparison to the sensation that is a result of
your lips pressing against mine

I am filled with *fascination*

awaiting to be blessed by s e r e n i t y

Let me ask you this, does your heart skip a beat and race simultaneously whenever you pass one of our spots? Does your stomach plunge to the floor each time I cross your mind? Tell me, do you still crave my presence the way you once did?

Because from my perspective, you don't even seem to miss me at all..

I'm slowly starting to process
one of the harshest realities I've had to face..

> she *is* indeed the love of my life
> I just may not be the love of hers
> despite how much I desire to be..

Your intuition combined
with your experiences
and knowledge gained
will help guide you
in the right direction
and find the path of life
you have been searching for

I am not proud of the mistakes I've made or the lies I've told
I have been trying to right my wrongs for quite some time now
but sometimes I want to just want to give up trying to be better
because even when I am truthful and genuinely trying to do better
no one believes me, but I suppose I dug my own grave
and I can't be mad at anyone, except my past self and her mistakes

I long for more than just a physical connection
I crave passion, depth, and intimacy

so before our bodies become skin-to-skin
our souls need time to meet

we ache for someone, just *anyone*
to even notice we are drowning
but when we see a hand
as it is reaching to save us
we refuse to grab it… *why?*

CREATE **SMILES**.

PROMOTE **LOVE**.

ENCOURAGE **AUTHENTICITY**.

-My personal life motto

One last reminder:

YOU ARE ENOUGH
YOU CAN RISE UP
YOU ARE STRONG
YOU MATTER

Please don't give up on yourself;
I believe in you!

Made in the USA
Las Vegas, NV
20 April 2021